Will's net

Story written by Cynthia Rider
Illustrated by Tim Archbold

Speed Sounds

Consonants   *Ask children to say the sounds.*

f	l	m	n	r	s	v	z	**sh**	**th**	ng
ff	ll		nn		ss	ve	zz			nk
							s			

b	c	d	g	h	j	p	qu	t	w	x	y	ch
bb	k		gg					tt	wh			tch
	ck											

Each box contains one sound but sometimes more than one grapheme.
*Focus graphemes for this story are **circled**.*

Vowels

Ask children to say the sounds in and out of order.

a	e	i	o	u
at	hen	in	on	up

ay	ee	igh	ow	oo
day	see	high	blow	zoo

Story Green Words

Ask children to read the words first in Fred Talk and then say the word.

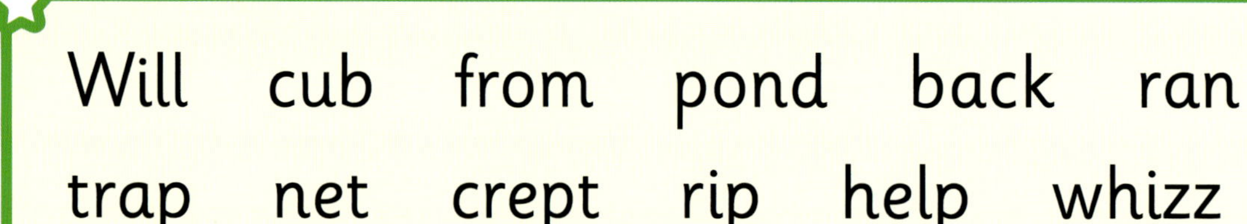

Will   cub   from   pond   back   ran

trap   net   crept   rip   help   whizz

Red Words

Ask children to practise reading the words across the rows, down the columns and in and out of order clearly and quickly.

said	the	I'll
to	no	bear*
I	he	be
your	do	my

** Red Word in this book only*

Will's net

Introduction

*Baby bears are called bear cubs. They love to eat fish.
Will is angry when a bear cub takes a fish from his pond.
So Will decides to catch the bear in his net, but the bear
doesn't want to be caught. Let's see what happens.*

A bear cub got a fish from Will's pond.

"Put it back!" said Will.

Grrr! went the cub ...

and Will ran.

"I'll get that cub!
I'll trap it
in a net,"
said Will.

Will crept back to the pond. *Whizz!*

Will got the cub in his net.
But the cub went *rip, rip, rip!*

"Help!" said Will.
"No net!"

Grrrr! went the cub and Will ran ...

and ran ...

and ran.

Questions to talk about

Ask children to TTYP for each question using 'Fastest finger' (FF) or 'Have a think' (HaT).

p.8 (HaT) How did Will feel about the cub catching a fish in his pond? (Look at the picture to help: pleased/cross/furious.)

p.9 (FF) What did the cub do?

p.10 (FF) What did Will decide to do?

How did Will get back to the pond?

p.11 (HaT) How did Will feel when the cub ripped through the net?

pp.12–13 (FF) What did he do?